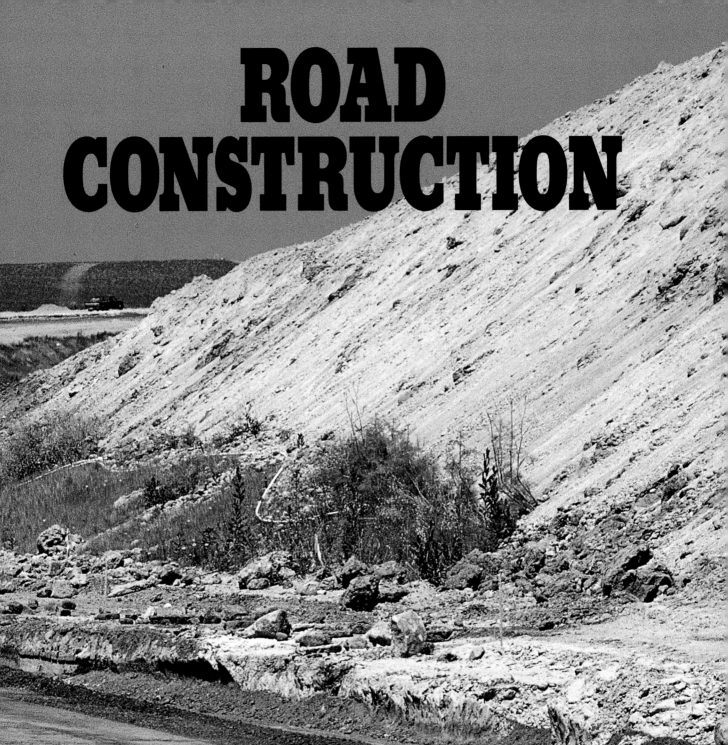

ROAD CONSTRUCTION

Robert Genat

Motorbooks International
Publishers & Wholesalers

I dedicate this book to my insightful friend, Jerry Stein.
He has helped me countless times without ever uttering a word of advice—
he knows how to ask the right questions.
Thanks for being such a good friend, Jerry.

◆

First published in 1995 by Motorbooks International Publishers & Wholesalers, PO Box 2, 729 Prospect Avenue, Osceola, WI 54020 USA

Motorbooks International books are also available at discounts in bulk quantity for industrial or sales-promotional use. For details write to Special Sales Manager at the Publisher's address

Library of Congress Cataloging-in-Publication Data
Genat, Robert.
    Road construction/Robert Genat.
        p. cm.––(Enthusiast color series)
    Includes index.
    ISBN 0-7603-0040-2 (pbk.)
    1. Road machinery. I. Title. II. Series.
TE223.G46   1995
625.7––dc20   95-17472

On the front cover: Canting this grader's front wheels helps the tires grip a slanted surface. *Robert Genat*

On the frontispiece: The elevated final drive sprocket on the CAT D8L is designed to be above the mud and dust and is isolated from the ground shocks absorbed by the treads. *Robert Genat*

On the title page: A spotless grader motors along on a road expansion job. *Robert Genat*

On the back cover: The bulldozer's blade is up and the operator is shifting into reverse after making a pass to the edge of a fill. *Robert Genat*

Printed in Hong Kong

Contents

Acknowledgments

My deepest gratitude to the wonderful men and women working in the road construction industry who helped me with this book. They gave me answers to "how's it work?", "what's that thing for?", and "why do you do it that way?". They let me climb on, in, and around several pieces of equipment. And they gave me rides on some of the equipment—that was fun!

A special thanks to John Daley of Daley Construction. When I told him of my project he invited me in, gave me a hard hat and an orange vest, and took me on a tour of his sites. I was given full access to all his sites and people. Thanks, John.

Thanks to Kirk Landers, editor of *Construction Equipment Magazine*. His publication is gospel to those in the industry. Writing this book would have been difficult without Kirk's help.

Thanks to all the equipment manufacturers for their cooperation. Not only do they build some of the toughest equipment in the world, but they're also some of the nicest folks in the country.

Introduction

One of the great things about being a little kid is playing with toys. And some of the most fondly remembered toys are the Tonka Toys. These bright yellow replicas of real, heavy equipment fired our imaginations. We tore up mom's flower beds on a regular basis with our land improvements and moved topsoil by the tiny bucket load. We could imitate the sounds of big motors, growling and screeching, as we crushed the azaleas and rolled over the petunias. We got dirty along with our big, tough toys. We all dreamed of running those large machines, whether it was a grader, an excavator or a bulldozer. Some dreams are never realized. We grow up to teach school, sell computers, or even write books. But, there are the lucky few who get to operate the big iron. They get to build America's roads and operate road construction equipment.

Each year, teams of huge, powerful machines move tons of earth and lay down thousands of cubic feet of concrete and asphalt. These earth sculptors can move tons of dirt with the grace of a dancer. They lay pavement as smooth as a billiard table. Millions of motorists travel along these well-constructed roads and highways, which link people to home, work, and play.

The road construction team consists of many players. Bulldozers are the tough guys that clear away tree stumps and level the ground. Excavators are the diggers. They cut, or remove, large amounts of soil and dig drainage lines. Scrapers come in next to cut and fill, meaning they remove soil from a high area and transport it to a low area. Graders follow as finishing machines. Their job is to give the dirt road its final, smooth finish prior to paving. Pavers do just that–they pave the road with asphalt or concrete. Rollers and compactors finish the job, ensuring that the road surface is smooth and reliable. We will also look at milling machines, which chew up old roads so they can be repaved.

So let's put on our hard hats, lace up our boots, and take a close-up look at these incredible pieces of equipment.

Chapter 1

A Brief History Of Roads— Where The Path Began

Man has always been a traveler, but prior to the invention of the wheel he had little need for roads. Footpaths were the highways of the day, and they were usually the shortest and easiest distance between two points. They only needed to be wide enough for one person, and elevation changes or turns of any degree were acceptable. These simple paths sufficed until the invention of the wheel created the need for roads. The wheel was probably invented between 3,000 and 4,000 B.C. and its use spread throughout Europe by 2,500 B.C., when wheels were commonly fitted to carts and chariots. The wheels were a great innovation. Unfortunately, few natural surfaces provide the proper texture for wheels to roll on, and the new wheels were tearing up the surfaces and causing ruts and pot holes (some problems never go away). Smoother, wider and more durable roads were needed.

A CAT 140G is making another pass down the road. This model is powered by a 150hp diesel and weighs in at close to 30,000lbs. The orange cone on the back covers a ripper that is turned up.

While the earliest roads can be traced as far back as 1500 B.C., the first architects of modern roads were the Romans. They built 50,000mi of roads between 300 B.C. and A.D. 300. The Roman roads were well-planned and beautifully built; many remain today. Roads were the key to the Roman's military and economic strength. Their major roads were as straight as possible, forty feet wide, had proper drainage, and were elevated about three feet above the surrounding land.

The first roads in America were a complex network of footpaths the Native Americans established between their villages and hunting grounds. Like the Romans, they routed their trails on high ground to give them a view of possible enemies or for scouting animals. When the Europeans settled in America, they brought the wheeled technology of the day; horse-drawn carts, carriages and wagons. Without roads, early penetration inland from the East Coast was limited to waterways. Beyond the waterways, there were the Allegheny mountains to conquer. Another major obstacle to road building was heavy foresta-

This large expanse of dirt is within days of becoming a freeway. String lines are set along the sides while the graders and rollers make their final passes. The excavation and preparation for paving is a lengthy process. It has taken over a year of work to prepare this grade.

tion. With all of the major cities on the Eastern seaboard connected by waterways, only the brave and adventurous went west. By the late 1700s, wider wagon paths were being cut through the coastal mountains. Clearing these paths was difficult as some of the trees stood 150ft tall. Thousands of years of fallen trees and shrubs made clearing the way even more laborious. Even after the path was cleared, wagons and carts required the high ground clearance provided by large diameter wheels to pass over remaining stumps and debris.

Because of the lack of coordination and dedication to road building by state and federal governments in the late 1700s, several private toll roads were set up in the fashion of English roads. These roads were called turnpikes because of the long pole called a "pike" that would be turned away after you paid your fee at the toll booth. In 1795, the Philadelphia and Lancaster Turnpike was opened. As the first major hard-surfaced road in America, the Philadelphia and Lancaster Turnpike's success triggered a boom in turnpike construction. Be-

De rigueur for today's construction worker: hard hat, orange vest with reflective stripes, and durable boots. While this worker does not drive a dozer (yet), she still has an important role on the road construction job site. She and her partner are in constant radio contact to control vehicle traffic in an area of a road expansion. Large dump trucks were maneuvering in and out of traffic after being loaded by an excavator. Traffic control is as much for the safety of the workers as for the auto travelers.

tween 1792 and 1828, Pennsylvania constructed over 3000mi of hard-surfaced roads.

The widespread use of the bicycle had an impact on roads. As new designs and improvements made bicycles safer and easier to ride, bicyclists saw the need for better roads. In 1890,

the voice of ten million bicyclists was heard through their organization, the League of American Wheelmen. Wielding power equal to today's Sierra Club, they fought for road improvements.

The single most important driving force behind road improvement was also the biggest revolution in modern society—the automobile. Initially seen as toys for the rich, automobiles became commonplace. In 1905, there were a total of seventy-eight thousand cars registered in the United States and twenty states had programs for the improvement of their roads. Also, between 1913 and 1916, there were several major pieces of federal and state legislation directed to highway construction. In 1925, a federal committee was formed to initiate a standard for road signs and markings. Until then each state had its own marking system, if it had one at all. The depression of the thirties initially slowed road construction. In 1933, the Civilian Construction Corps employed close to three hundred thousand men in many public works projects, including those devoted to road building.

In 1921, there were 3.2 million miles of roads. By 1961, that figure had jumped to 3.6 million miles. Today, our network of roads and streets is over 3.9 million miles long. It must be noted that a large percentage of the roads existing in 1921 were unimproved. It wasn't until 1943 that the number of surfaced roads (including gravel and stone) equaled the number of unimproved roads. By 1972, eighty percent of our roads were improved (meaning they were surfaced in some fashion). Today, over ninety-three percent of our roads are improved. Of that figure,

There must be an axiom for overcrowded roads. No matter how wide they are, motorists will fill them to capacity.

one-third are stone or gravel. We have come a long way to support our automotive habit. That habit includes 190 million registered motor vehicles being driven by 173 million drivers.

Each day, Americans travel almost four billion miles. We depend on roads for commerce and recreation. Good roads don't just happen, they are the result of good planning and engineering. Designing a road is like working out a difficult puzzle. How many cars will travel the road, how fast will they be going, and how do we preserve the natural environment. Vehicle dynamics and human dynamics also determine the design of the road. A 12ft lane width is considered a minimum. Rural roads have lane widths of between 13 and 14ft. Once a lane exceeds 14ft in width, drivers will try to squeeze in two cars. The maximum grade of a road should be no more than fifteen percent with a much lower amount of four to six percent being the accepted standard. Modern ve-

The Eighth Wonder of the World

"The Eighth Wonder of the World" is how the Pennsylvania Turnpike was touted at its opening on October 1, 1940. "The Pike," as it was called by locals, stretched 160mi from Middlesex to Irwin. This was America's first superhighway, but it had its skeptics. Many said that few would use it. Even the U.S. Bureau of Roads predicted that only 700 cars per day would travel the Pike. Actual use for the first two weeks was approximately 10,000 cars per day. Motorists traveled its four lanes of concrete at speeds as high as 90mph. Long, gentle curves provided easy entrance and exit. A 10ft wide grassy median separated the lanes of traffic. Service stations and restaurants were conveniently spaced. This was a glimpse of the future—high speed automobile travel.

The dream was shattered as the first fatality occurred three weeks after opening. Vehicle speeds were dangerously high, and drivers complained of being lulled into a hypnotic trance by the long stretches of featureless straight road. A 70mph speed limit was set within a year, and guard rails started to pop up along the narrow median.

The Pennsylvania Turnpike is America's oldest surviving superhighway. It now stretches 360mi between the Ohio Turnpike and the New Jersey Turnpike. In its lifetime it has carried well over two billion vehicles and will continue to carry vehicles well into the twenty-first century.

---

hicles can climb grades of ten percent without too much difficulty. The designed slope for a modern road is between 1/4 to 1/2in per foot. The amount of slope is determined by the type of material. Concrete has the least amount of slope, and dirt roads have the most.

Human dynamics are also important to the design of a road. Human reaction time is critical to the safety of a road. One engineer, speaking of today's drivers said, "attentiveness is more important than intelligence." Today's driver is most content with consistency of design, standard lane widths, markings, and signage. Signs are the same size and shape from state to state. Most shoulders are designed with a different color than the traffic lane. This contrast gives the driver a visual cue to the lane boundaries, especially at night.

Chapter 2

Bulldozers—The Tough Guys

The bulldozer is probably the most identifiable piece of construction equipment in the world. More commonly called "dozers", they are the go-anywhere, do-anything members of the construction team. Along with the excavator, dozers are the first mechanized pieces of equipment to arrive at a new construction site. Transportation of a dozer to and from the job site is a tricky proposition because of their size. Dozers must be transported by truck because they can weigh as much as 200,000lbs and their steel cleat treads would tear up any road . The trailers used to transport these monsters are specially built on a very low platform with multiple sets of tires to spread the load out evenly. The low platform is required because of the height of the loaded dozer. You certainly can't miss them on the road as they are pulled by a diesel tractor and accompanied by additional vehicles with "wide load" warning signs.

This Cat D8L pushes its 285hp into a cut, while the water truck in the background lays down a spray of water. Watering reduces dust loosens the soil.

Once at the site, the dozer's task is to prepare the area for the scrapers and graders. The wide crawler treads allow the dozers to climb steep hills and traverse areas unsuitable for less agile pieces of equipment. The dozers power through the site, removing tree stumps and leveling the ground. They do heavy cutting with their front blade, also called a dozer. This may entail removal of an entire hill or simply dozing trees and shrubs. With their blade, they remove organic growth that would be an unsuitable base for a paved road. They may cut into areas and then pile that dirt up near an excavator to be loaded and hauled away. Or they may push it to a low area that needs to be filled. With their high horsepower (up to 1,000hp) and crawler treads, bulldozers have the ability to pull out stumps and deep roots with their blade or with rippers. Rippers are long sharp steel teeth mounted on the rear of the dozer which can be hydraulically raised and lowered. The operator drives forward and activates a control lever to lower the rippers. The ends of the rippers are curved to help them burrow into the ground as they are pulled along. The rippers break up soil

The slope cutter on this Cat D8L is retracted. Judging from the rust build-up on the cutter, it hasn't been used as frequently as the sand-polished blade or rippers. Compare the size of the massive rippers to that of the operator.

that has been compacted over the years and snaps old tree roots like twigs. A pass or two with these sharp rippers leaves the soil loose enough so the scrapers can move in to pick it up.

A dozer also eliminates the need for a tow truck on the construction site. If any of the wheeled equipment gets bogged down due to soft soil or mud, the dozer will come to the rescue. It is not unusual to see a dozer pushing a scraper that bogged down in the middle of his cut. The dozer's large crawler treads allow it to easily push its buddy out.

Driving a dozer is no picnic; the ride is rough. Driving over unimproved land covered with stumps and large rocks can be a jarring event. Treads are designed for traction, not a smooth ride. Most cabs are open and the operator is exposed to all types of weather conditions as well as the dust kicked up by the blade.

From the operator's thickly padded seat the view is excellent. Displayed in front of the operator is a no-nonsense instrument panel with a minimum of gauges and warning lights. To the right of the instrument panel is the

The large pair of rippers on the back of this dozer are controlled by two pairs of hydraulic cylinders. One set lowers and raises the rippers and the other set changes their angle of attack. The tips and leading edges are replaceable.

throttle lever, which is used to set engine rpm. Speed is controlled with the decelerator pedal on the floorboard. The hand throttle sets the power level and the decelerator reduces power. The dozer is normally run with the hand throttle set for maximum power. As the operator applies pressure on the decelerator, power to the treads is reduced and the dozer slows. In this way, the operator regulates the speed of the dozer. While driving down a hill, for ex-

ample, the operator would press the pedal to keep the dozer's speed low. To stop, the operator depresses the decelerator and brake at the same time.

The bulldozer has no steering wheel, just a pair of levers on the left console. These two levers turn the dozer by reducing power to either the right or left tread. If you pull back on the right hand lever, the dozer will turn right as the right tread slows down and the

17

A dozer and its rippers leaves a path of
devastation and destruction. Loosened soil is
then easily picked up by a scraper.

Right, this dozer operator is backing up. His left hand is on the left tread steering control and his right foot is on the decelerator.

Bottom, this is the flight deck of a Cat D4H. Visibility from this elevated platform is very good. Both edges of the blade are visible as are both treads. The comfortable seat is covered with black vinyl. The pair of levers on the left controls steering. The smaller single lever controls direction and gear choice. Two pedals are on the floor: the pedal on the left is the brake and the pedal on the right is the decelerator. The lever above the decelerator is the throttle. The horizontal grip on the right is the dozer control, and just behind it is the ripper control.

As the dozer is moving forward, the water truck comes alongside to water down the area being dozed.

left tread attempts to pass it by. If you pull back all the way on the right lever, it will lock the right tread and you will spin on a dime to the right. The lever on the left performs the same function for the left tread.

The transmission power shifter is to the left of the steering controls. This lever selects forward or reverse direction and gear selection in each range. The dozer or blade control lever and the ripper control lever are on the console to the driver's right. The movement of the rippers is controlled by the simple up and down motion of the lever. The dozer control lever is handled with the touch of a skilled artisan. This lever controls the cutting and must be constantly adjusted as the operator moves

Also note the elevated drive sprocket, a fairly new feature that decreases wear by elevating the drive sprocket above the dirt and grime and isolating it from the pounding of the ground.

along. This lever may also control the angle or tilt of the blade.

While the controls for a dozer are relatively simple, handling one of these beasts is not. Skilled operators possess good hand-eye (and foot-eye) coordination and an uncanny ability to make minute adjustments and keep the blade peeling off the correct amount of turf. Once the blade is down and digging in, it's up to the operator's skill and feel. The only visual cue is the amount of dirt spilling off the blade. He must also feel the attitude of the machine and carefully adjust the power

using the decelerator. When one side of the blade digs in, the dozer will skew out of its intended path without a precise amount of steering correction. The operator must be able to feel the amount of power needed and know the type of material being moved. Different soil types, general topography, and hazards determine each move. All of the senses come into play to interpret what is happening to the machine and adjust the proper control to maintain the cut.

In addition, some dozers come equipped with optional foot steering. Skilled opera-

The rippers on the back of this Cat D4H are much smaller than the ones on its big brother, the D8L.

tors switch between foot and hand controls as easily as we switch from a Ford to a Chevy.

The life of a bulldozer and it's operator is a tough one. They are the first on scene and get the tough job of preparing the land for the excavators and scrapers to follow. The powerful machines and highly skilled dozer operators make turning nasty terrain into the beginnings of smooth highways look as easy as a Sunday drive.

The slope cutter is laid down parallel with the
bottom edge of the blade, effectively widening
the blade for this pass.

Left, this Cat D9H has been superseded by the D9N that uses the elevated sprocket design. Today's duty has been to push mud around and quite a bit is stuck on the sides and treads. One cannot appreciate the mass and power of these machines without a close-up look at how well they are built.

Above, at over 40 tons, moving a large Cat D8L is no easy task. Large custom trailers are used for transport. The trailers have six axles full of wheels to spread the heavy load. They are slung low to provide bridge clearance.

Chapter 3

Excavators—Digging For Dollars

Like dozers, excavators are one of the first pieces of heavy equipment to arrive on scene. Years ago, they were called steam shovels because of their steam power and shovel at the end of the long arm. The shovel, or bucket, remains, but today's excavators are diesel-powered and computer-controlled. An excavator's undercarriage is capped off by a pair of large crawler treads. These treads give the excavator mobility in undeveloped terrain. The design of the undercarriage allows the carbody above to swivel 360deg. The carbody contains the diesel engine, hydraulic pumps, and cab for the operator. Attached to the carbody is the boom, the first of the two portions of the arm. The boom is shaped like a boomerang and at its far end is attached the stick. The stick extends out and at its end is the bucket. Boom and stick combinations can provide a reach of over sixty feet. An example of where that long reach could be used is in

Right, wow—a close look at the two cubic yards of dirt that was just dumped.

Left, this is what two cubic yards of dirt look like when they is scooped up by this excavator's bucket.

Above, this excavator operator's left hand is on the left joystick that controls the swing and stick movement. The stick is the end portion of the arm to which the bucket attaches.

Right, the big Cats get thirsty, too. Custom-built trucks bring not only fuel, but a daily dose of preventive medicine in the form of grease for all the zerk fittings. Preventive maintenance is the key to machine longevity. These trucks and their operators do a tremendous service to their contractors.

Above, looking like a Jurassic Park clash of prehistoric buckets, two excavators work together.

Left, once again, the combined work of giants. The dozer is pushing the wet clay into the area of the excavator. Because the scraper is unable to work with this type of soil, the excavator is loading the scraper. The scraper will then transport his load to another part of the site.

The boom and stick of this Komatsu excavator give it a reach of over 35ft. The worker on the ground has temporarily stopped traffic on this road and is watching the graceful arc of this versatile machine.

river conservation or dredging where light loads are handled at extended distances. Shorter length combinations provider greater digging and lifting power while sacrificing reach.

At the end of the stick is the bucket, which does the digging. Buckets are rated in cubic yards of capacity and range in size from .75 to 10.5 cubic yards (you could easily park a Corvette in a 10.5 cubic yard bucket). Other accessories are available as a replacement for the bucket, such as roller compactors and special-

ized demolition attachments. A system of high pressure hydraulics ties the boom, stick, and bucket together, all controlled by the operator.

Excavators come in multitude of sizes, with over 190 different new models available. Various combinations of weight, horsepower, digging depth, and bucket size match any application. Excavators range in horsepower from 85 to 650. Operating weights range from the little guys at 26,780lbs to the sumo wrestler size of 213,000lbs. Other variables are maximum digging depth and buck-

Under the back of this Komatsu PC300LC is a six-cylinder 207hp diesel engine. This engine runs the hydraulic pumps that make this beast such a hard worker. Notice the large neatly plumbed hydraulic lines running up the boom (the boomerang shaped portion of the arm).

et size. With a multitude of options available, the contractor can tailor the excavator to exact job needs.

The excavator arrives early to the job site, usually brought in by the same type of truck that hauls other heavy equipment like the bulldozer. Excavators are used for road construction when there is an abundance of soil to be removed (cutting) or drainage lines to be dug. Undeveloped areas demand equip-

Notice the interesting wear strips welded onto the side of the bucket in the foreground. Many contractors will have their company name welded into the pattern to reduce theft.

Contractors occasionally arrive at their job site in the morning only to find one of their buckets missing.

ment with mobility and the excavator's crawler treads allow them to traverse almost any terrain. The excavators may be used to uproot trees and move large boulders which would hamper or prohibit the movement of other wheeled equipment.

Excavators will also be used to move large areas which need to be cut or removed. This may be a large hill which will be chipped away at for weeks or months. To accomplish

this, a dozer will first clear a path to give access for the trucks to be loaded. The excavator will then position itself to efficiently load those trucks. As it works away on the cut of the hill, the excavator will continually adjust its position between the trucks and the area to be cut. In some areas, a dozer will use its blade to push soil to the excavator for loading.

Another use of excavators in road construction is the digging of drainage lines. First,

The versatility of these machines is again shown. The bucket has a cable attached and is lifting old pipe out of the ground. Notice the artistic pattern of wear strips that have been welded onto the bucket.

This is an operator's view of the world. Depth perception is a necessity for an operator. Today's task is to dig trenches for lay drainage pipe.

the excavator trenches the path for the pipe. Once the trench is dug, the excavator can lay the pipe. This is done by wrapping a cable around the pipe and attaching it to the bucket. Once the pipe is in place, the excavator fills the trench and covers the pipe.

The excavation of a road construction site will generally require a bucket of some type. The most common buckets used are for digging, and they come in a variety of types. General purpose buckets perform routine, everyday excavation and dirt digging. Heavy-duty buckets are used to dig in rougher conditions, such as light rock and dense clay. For highly abrasive applications such as heavy rock and demolition, there are severe-duty buckets. Bucket widths usually come in increments of six inches.

Scraper's wheels can easily get stuck in soft or wet soil. This bogged-down scraper is being helped out of its predicament by an excavator. The entire operation was like watching a mother lion with her cub. The excavator operator smoothly, carefully, and gently helped its friend out of the mire.

Buckets are a high-wear item because of the constant digging into all sorts of substances. Repeated contact with sharp rocks takes it toll on the condition of the bucket. In order to prolong a bucket's useful life, most contractors weld rub strips onto the areas most vulnerable to excessive wear, such as the sides, to improve durability. Rub strips are nothing more than a series of weld beads added along these high-wear areas. The rub strips may have the contractor's name as part of the pattern to help de-

ter theft. The last thing a contractor wants is to arrive at the job site to find an excavator bucket missing. The teeth at the leading edge of the bucket are replaceable, since digging into rock will break them off occasionally.

Excavator operators must have excellent depth perception in order to keep everything within range of the bucket. Excellent peripheral vision is necessary for the operator as he swings the bucket. The operator must be aware of all elements in this potentially hazardous environment. Tons of dirt at the end of a swinging arm could seriously damage another piece of equipment or injure or kill a bystander. A heavy bucketful swinging in what could be a radius of over 60ft make's for a dangerous place to work. Skillful operators dig with ease. They use a smooth, rhythmic motion of scooping, swinging, unloading, and returning to dig again. The motion is much like the graceful arms of a dancer as opposed to the jerky movements of a robot. Smooth acceleration and deceleration of the bucket swing are essential for efficient work. Operators must dig with care to avoid undercutting their own footing and falling into the hole they have just dug. Good operators are also aware of the type of soil and its limitations. Poor judgment on the operator's part may put him in an area too steep to dig on and still swing the arm safely. Improper location may cause the excavator to tip over. The operator needs to be sure of his location so as not to undercut his own footing.

Sophisticated digital controls help the operator with his work. Hydraulic excavators have been widely used since the sixties, whereas computer controls have been added only within the past ten years. The newer, state-of-the-art excavators allow the operator to select the hydraulic pump output to maximize speed and economy. All of this is done with the touch of a button from the seat of the cab. Most new excavators have two or three power selection levels. While each manufacturer has its own specific name for each power mode, they are usually broken down like this: a general mode for normal digging and loading; a heavy-duty mode for difficult work, such as digging in rocky areas where high horsepower is essential; and a fine lifting mode where smooth movements are critical. These modes can be changed with the touch of a button without interrupting the flow of work.

Critical to the addition of these controls is the electronics that drive them. The temperature extremes and vibration excavators are subjected to would destroy unprotected electronics, so the circuitry must be shock-mounted and protected from the elements. Many excavators have override systems that allow standard digging if the selected system fails.

One excellent addition to the electronics package is built-in electronic troubleshooting. This diagnostic equipment is similar to the equipment auto mechanics use on modern cars. The service technician can just plug in and diagnose a problem in minutes, instead of hours. The advantage here is that the mechanic makes his diagnosis at the job site.

Options abound to enhance the operator's working environment. Cabs are spacious and user-friendly. Operator comfort is directly related to production and safety. Most of the newer models offer cloth-covered eight-way adjustable seats. The armrests, with hand controllers at the end, are independently adjustable from the seat. This allows each operator to use the controls for maximum comfort and control. And yes, air-conditioning is available, along with oscillating fans, seat belts, heater, and AM/FM radio.

The excavator is a very versatile machine. It combines power with the ability to

This Komatsu PC220LC is laying its 50,000lbs of weight into this compaction tool. The back and forth action of this tool is not unlike cutting a pizza with a rotary cutter. Notice how the front edges of the treads are off the ground. Have I said that an excavator is versatile?

move over the roughest terrain. It offers the contractor a flexible tool with the capacity to dig drainage trenches, lay pipe, and do large cutting. Its computerized controls aid the skilled operator in completing his tasks in minimal time. Excavators prepare the land for the next phase of road construction and for the next group of machines in line.

Right, with extreme concentration and a joystick in each hand, this excavator operator is pulling up another bucketful. A loss of concentration with this machine could cause thousands of dollars of damage or loss of life.

Chapter 4

Scrapers—Push-Pull Production

One of the fastest pieces of road construction equipment is the scraper. Its massive horsepower (200 to 700) and large wheels make it capable of speeds up to 35mph. Like shotguns, scrapers come in single-barrel and double-barrel versions. A single-barrel has a single engine in the front. Double-barrel scrapers have two large diesel engines, one in the front and one in the rear. The front portion of a scraper is called the "tractor" while the rear portion is called the "scraper." The operator and controls are located in the tractor. The scraper contains the bowl, sometimes called the "can." This is where the scraped dirt is held.

Scrapers are articulated, meaning that the tractor and the bowl are attached with a hinge. The wheels are solidly mounted and the scraper turns by bending at the hinge, which allows a tight turning radius.

Maximum capacity for a large scraper's bowl is forty-four cubic yards, but the average scraper generally holds about twenty-five cu-

Coming at you in the early morning light, this scraper moves across a well-worn path.

bic yards. There are also scrapers with a larger capacity designed to haul coal.

Scrapers are brought in after the dozers and excavators have smoothed the area. The scraper's job is to cut and fill, that is, to remove soil from a high area and quickly move it to fill a low area. The cut is made by lowering the bowl into the ground. The front edge of the bowl has a full-width horizontal cutting edge made of replaceable hardened steel sectional plates. At each end of the cutting edge are vertical plates called "slobber bits." Slobber bits are the visual aids for the operator to gauge the depth of cut.

Here's how the hardware works. There are three levers to the operator's right: the bowl control, the apron control, and the ejector. The bowl control lowers and raises the bowl, determining the amount of cut. The apron is a sliding door which drops down over the open front of the bowl, keeping the freshly scraped dirt inside. The ejector is a large ram on a telescoping hydraulic cylinder that pushes the dirt out of the bowl when dumping the fill dirt into a low area. The width of the bowl provides for an even application of the fill material.

Two Cat 637Ds in the "push" phase of a push-pull cut. The operator in the lead scraper has just lowered his bowl to cut. The operator in the rear has already floored his accelerators to help his buddy with the cut.

The lead scraper has already filled his bowl with the help of his friend pushing from the rear. Now it's time for him to return the favor by pulling his buddy through his cut.

Left, with a quick look back, the operator can see that his bowl is filled and spilling over the side. His right hand is on the control to close the apron and lift the bowl above ground level to stop the cut.

This battle-scarred Cat 637 has probably moved millions of tons in its lifetime. Properly maintained, these machines can be effective tools for many years. Good operators take the time to pre-flight their machine prior to the work day. A simple mechanical breakdown can cause delays that cost a contractor thousands of dollars.

Let's ride along as the operator positions the scraper in the area of the cut. First he will shift around in his seat to look over his right shoulder at the slobber bits. With his left hand on the steering wheel and his right hand on the bowl control lever, he will drop the bowl to the appropriate depth for the cut. While the scraper can cut as deep as 18in, the average cut is usually about six inches, depending on the conditions. With the depth set, the power comes on, and the cut is made. The operator's eyes are on the slobber bits and the filling bowl with an occasional glance in the direction of travel. Once the bowl is filled, the apron will be dropped and the bowl raised. Then the operator will quickly drive along the haul road to the

Cat helping Cat as a D8L dozer powers 285hp into its crawler treads to help a scraper with its cut.

fill area. The advantage of the large rubber tires and high speed is reduced travel time to the fill area. Maximum speed for a scraper is around 35mph on level ground. After arriving at the fill area, the driver will open the apron and activate the ejector to empty the bowl. As the operator drives forward, the load is spread along his path creating the fill. I asked one operator about the most dangerous aspect of driving a scraper. "Speed," was his first reply. He then went on to clarify how fast a scraper can accelerate on a downhill haul road with a full

45

With a quick glance at his buddies cutting in the background, this scraper operator is coming back from filling to take another cut.

load. An inexperienced operator can let it get away from him. An operator has to be careful in the area of a fill. The soil is not compacted and if you are on the edge of the fill the scraper can go over. The operator I spoke to once rolled a scraper down a hill and broke his back.

One advantage of scrapers is that they are designed to be worked together in a "push–pull" configuration. Push-pull is where two scrapers, properly equipped, team up to help each other. Every scraper has a stinger— an extended push bar—on the back of the scraper to provide an area for another piece

Scraper operators spend a majority of their time looking over their right shoulder at the front edge of the bowl, watching the cut.

While not able to turn on the proverbial dime, the scraper can make a very tight turn. The tractor, or front section, can turn ninety degrees to the bowl or rear section.

of equipment, such as a dozer, to push them if they get stuck. In push-pull, the stinger on one scraper is pushed by the tractor of a second scraper. The scraper doing the pushing has a large push-plate on the front. As scraper one is cutting, scraper two is pushing from behind. This exerts the total horsepow- er from four diesel engines driving through eight large tires. While scraper two is push- ing, the operator is lowering his scraper's bail (a hinged bar in the shape of a half hoop) on the front, to latch onto a hook on the back of scraper one's stinger. When scraper one's bowl is filled and raised, scraper two's bowl

Above, this welder is in the jaws of the monster, attaching a new "slobber bit." Welded to the edge of the bowl, slobber bits are what the operators watch to gauge the depth of cut. The large horizontal piece behind the welder is the edge that is lowered to make the cut.

Right, having just dumped his load, this operator is taking advantage of the horsepower of two large diesels and a smooth area. At 35mph, the scraper has the highest speed of all road construction vehicles. Operators will tell you that the speeds get much higher when you have both a full bowl and both throttles floored while going down a steep haul-road.

The dozer is going north with its rippers down, loosening the ground. The scrapers are coming in for a southerly pass to make their cut across previously ripped ground.

Two large Cat scrapers coming at you. The lead scraper is pulling the scraper in the rear. Notice how the driver sits at an angle in his seat so he can keep a constant watch over his right shoulder. Also note that the push plate in the front of this machine has fresh grease on it, indicating he has been a puller all day.

It's not unusual to have a scraper loaded by an excavator. This area has a lot of clay and the scrapers would otherwise get bogged down.

Just after filling his bowl, the front machine is helping his buddy in the rear by pulling him along. There is no radio communication between operators. Experienced operators work together smoothly without verbal communication.

will be lowered, and scraper two will be pulled by scraper one to help with his cut. Again, four motors and eight tires are helping with the cut. As scraper two finishes his cut, he will accelerate slightly, releasing the tension off his bail, and retract it thereby unhooking the two scrapers. He will give a small wiggle to indicate to operator one that he is free, and they will both motor down the haul road to dump their load. The operator of the rear scraper has the most responsibility, since he can see both machines. Watching two skilled operators in push-pull is like watching operations on the flight deck of an aircraft carrier. Everything is smoothly choreographed, with no wasted motion and minimum communication.

Scrapers are valued for their ability to move large amounts of dirt quickly when cutting and filling. They have the ability to team up and double the amount of power needed to make their cuts. They provide a key step in road building by providing the fill base needed for good roads.

In this profile of a Cat 623B tractor, you can clearly see one of the two large hydraulic cylinders that steer this beast ninety degrees to each side. Also note the Medusa-like group of hydraulic lines that control the scraper's hydraulically operated bowl, apron, and ejector functions. The white box on top of the cab is the air conditioner, a luxury option.

The scraper chassis is also used as a water tanker. The tank that replaces the bowl holds thousands of gallons of water. Sprayers mounted on the front and rear and both sides are operated independently of each other. Water blasts out at a pressure high enough to injure anyone standing too close. Water is used to control dust and to aid in soil compaction of a fill area.

Chapter 5

Graders—Earth Sculptors

As a kid, I was always most impressed by graders. Maybe it was their long wheel base, high cab, or large rear driving wheels. Maybe it's the fact they can push large amounts of soil or carefully cut a fraction of an inch off of a grade. Whatever it is, they still fascinate me.

A grader is a large wheeled machine. The basic layout has the large diesel engine over the four rear driving wheels. In front of the engine is the high mounted cab. Extending in front of the cab is the backbone portion of the frame, to which the blade is attached. Up front at the end of the backbone are the two steerable front wheels.

The average road grader varies from 26 to slightly over 32ft in length. They are supported by six large tires similar to those used on the scraper. The rear portion is supported by four of those tires, and they provide the driving force for operation. The diesel engine that drives those wheels sits above and ranges between 125 and 275hp. The grader's work is less arduous and therefore does not require the higher horsepower of their dozer and scraper brothers.

In front of the engine is the cab, which looks like nothing more than a glass box. From the cab, the operator steers and operates the controls for the blade. The front tires can be leaned up to eighteen degrees to keep the grader balanced on a slope. In addition to the front wheels turning and leaning, the entire front assembly can be articulated by a frame pivot just behind the cab. Articulation allows the front portion of the frame to pivot from side to side independent of the turning of the front wheels. This articulation, by turning the frame and wheels in the same direction, allows for easier blading on narrow roads or sharp turns. The frame can be articulated, turned one direction (left for instance), and the wheels turned to the opposite direction (to the right), to set up a crab path where front and rear wheels are following a parallel track. This technique would be used for cutting banks and side slopes.

This spotless grader is motoring along on a road expansion job. The dirt flowing off the heel of the blade is being piled into a windrow. His next pass will work down that windrow.

This vintage Allis-Chalmers grader is being used to spread asphalt over a midwestern rural road. Today's graders have hydraulically actuated steering as opposed to this older model's manual steering.

In the past, graders were operated a majority of the time with the operator standing. Today, graders are designed for more comfortable operation from a seated position. Adjustable control consoles bring the control levers within easy reach of the operator. In the center of this console is a conventional steering wheel. On each side are a series of closely spaced blade control levers which are logically placed for one-hand operation. The operator has two hydraulic pump settings. Normal operation will use 2150psi and for heavy duty operation he will select 3500psi. Advances in hydraulic pump technology allow the driver smooth control of the blade regardless of engine speed. Blade control is what this machine is all about. The blade, or moldboard assembly, has an infinite amount of adjustments. The angle of attack can be changed, the blade can be raised or lowered, angled to cut on either side, shifted off-center to place the blade to one side of the grader, or any combination of the above.

The grader can have an optional rear-mounted ripper attachment much like the one on the rear of the bulldozer. The shanks of the rippers are much smaller than those of the dozer. The grader's lack of horsepower and traction are the limiting factors. The rippers are used in the same fashion as the dozer. They are dropped into the soil and dragged

Front wheel lean is evident in this photo. This feature helps the grader keep its footing on a slanted surface.

along to break up the compacted dirt. The grader can then make a pass over the same area with its blade to plow away the freshly turned soil.

The grader's primary use is as a finishing machine. They are the last machines to travel the road prior to paving. They work closely with the compactors to achieve the "Boston gloss" or final smooth road. The compactors will travel over the area running their vibrating drums to compact the soil. As it is compacted, the soil will compress at dissimilar rates in different areas. This will cause high and low spots. This is where the grader comes in to take down the high spots and fill in the low areas. The operator's skill in being able to cut fractions of an inch off the grade is the key to the success of this operation. The compactor will come in again, and the process will be repeated over and over until the foundation for the road is smooth and ready for paving.

The grader is a versatile, bladed road construction machine. Precise controls over the blade give the grader its ability to create smooth roads. In conjunction with the compactors they provide the solid base for a new road.

Like soldiers standing at attention, the rippers on the back of this grader are turned up and out of the way. The replaceable tip can be clearly seen. As evidenced by the surface rust, these guys have not been used in a while.

Years ago, driving a grader was done while standing. Today's controls are adjustable, enabling the operator to sit, thus reducing fatigue. Another comfort feature is air conditioning. The six levers to the left of the steering wheel represent only half of the blade controls, the other six are to the right of the wheel.

A Cat 140G is making another pass down the road. This model is powered by a 150hp diesel and weighs in at close to 30,000lbs. The orange cone on the back covers a ripper that is turned up.

I almost got a little too close on this one, as the heel of the passing blade spills dirt in my direction.

The worker with the shovel is directing the grader operator. Deep in the ground just to the right of the worker's shovel is a grade stake. It has blue plastic feathers on top and its depth is set to establish the proper grade. The worker indicates to the operator how much to cut in order to get down to grade; in this instance, only a fraction of an inch is needed.

Right, the "doctor" is making a house call. This grader has lost a hydraulic seal in its moldboard actuating cylinder. Hydraulic fluid is visible on the back of the moldboard and on the rear tire. Not fully visible in the cab is the operator; he's the one with the concerned look on his face.

Chapter 6

Milling Machines—A Cut Above

One of the meanest machines used in road construction, or should I say road re-construction, is the "asphalt eater," formally known as a milling machine, cold planer, or pavement profiler. Milling machines are large, track-driven vehicles that have a large drum cutter underneath. Milling machines are used for removing asphalt, concrete, or soil. They chew up and spit out pavement at a torrid pace. Milling machines prepare an existing road in need of repair for a new layer of pavement. They also can expand a current road by removing the shoulder in preparation for new pavement. This milling action removes the top layer of concrete or asphalt. Lumps in the road created by years of weather and stress are smoothed out.

The key to the milling machine's operation is a large revolving drum containing hundreds of replaceable tungsten carbide teeth. This drum is brought into contact with the

Down the road our milling machine goes, leaving a rough looking, but smooth and properly graded surface on which the paver will lay a new mat of asphalt. A street sweeper is coming into view to pick up stray debris to prevent it from entering the nearby traffic lane.

pavement and cuts the surface to a new grade. The number of teeth on the drum is determined by the size of the machine and the diameter of the drum. The rotating drum is lowered onto and into the pavement, and the machine is driven forward. Crawler tracks provide the drive. The tracks provide traction against the action of the cutter, which rotates opposite the direction of travel. The cutters remove pavement in the same fashion as does a machine shop's horizontal milling machine. Each machine contains grade controls to maintain the depth of cut and angle of slope. The cutters are constantly cooled by water spray, and the milled roadway is fed up a conveyor system to waiting dump trucks.

The conveyor system is designed to swing from side to side. This aids in maneuverability and loading of trucks. The key to keeping a milling machine working is having a truck in position to accept its output of ground-up pavement. Where space will allow, two trucks are positioned side-by-side at the end of the conveyor. After the first is filled, it leaves, and the conveyor is swung over to the second truck. As it is filling, another truck is moved into the

The camera's strobe light freezes the spinning cutter drum exposing some of the 152 teeth on this Roadtec RX-45. The cutter drum rotates against the direction of travel. The conveyor belt lowers with the cutter drum to transport the debris up to a waiting dump truck.

Milled asphalt road shoots off the end of the 32in wide conveyor into the bed of a waiting truck. Note the two small red air horns on the end of the conveyor. A quick beep of these horns signals the truck driver to pull ahead slightly as the conveyor edges close to the back of the truck bed while the milling machine inches forward.

position of the first and so on. Where traffic restrictions will not allow trucks to be positioned side-by-side, individual trucks are maneuvered into position directly in front of the machine. This changing of trucks is the only thing that slows the progress of a milling machine. If the work being done is in an open area, the debris can be piled up and later scooped into dump trucks with a front loader. Pavement profilers can grind up thousands of tons of asphalt road per day to be recycled into another road.

These bad boys come in two basic configurations of crawler track design: three-track and four-track. The three-track design has a pair of tracks in the front and a single track in

The operator's gloved hand eases the lever ahead, controlling forward velocity. The cutting speed is measured in feet-per-minute (fpm), with a maximum fpm of 120. The large red push button is an emergency shutdown.

Right, negotiating a turn can be tricky. This Roadtec has a 20ft turn radius with the front track only and a 12ft turn radius using both front and rear. Notice how high this planer is raised for maneuvering.

This RX-45, with its 86in wide cutter, is classified as a medium-sized machine. It's hard to imagine anything over 45ft long, almost 15ft high with over 400hp as being "medium-size."

the rear. Four-track models are the largest and are arranged with two pairs of tracks, front and rear. Steering is done with the front track or both front and rear tracks. With the ability to steer both sets of tracks, the turning radius can be almost half that of a turn with only a single set. While watching one being positioned on a downtown street, it was interesting to observe the operator negotiate a tight intersection. He was turning with both the front and rear tracks and moving the conveyor from side to side at the same time. This balancing act was execut-

Dual stations allow the operator to work from either side. The ride is a bit bumpy as the cutters eat up the pavement below.

ed without damage to surrounding property or to his machine. Tracks can be crab steered for tight quarters maneuvering or cutting. The largest four-track models are over 50ft long and 14ft high. Maximum weight is over 100,000lbs. Cutting speed is measured in feet-per-minute and can be as high as 120, working out to about 1.3mph. The factor that determines the speed is the depth of cut and the type of material being cut. Maximum cut depth is 12in. Maximum speed while not milling is a little over 4mph.

Asphalt eaters are big money savers for a community. No longer is it necessary to dig up and replace an entire street. The top layer of the street can be milled off (and recycled) and a new layer of pavement applied. This technology has extended to very specialized large milling machines with self-contained pavers. In this case, the old road material removed, processed, and mixed with additional new hot mix and then laid back down by the same machine. The ultimate recycling machine!

Next page, outside Chicago, this CMI PR-800-7 is making its way north as traffic speeds past. Working on major highways is a dangerous proposition. Traffic lanes need to be closed to complete the work. Everything possible is done to alleviate traffic congestion, but motorists continue to speed through. Due to the danger to workers, several states have doubled speeding fines in road construction areas.

Chapter 7

Pavers—Laying It Down

Ninety-three percent of America's roads are of asphalt construction. That equates to over 3.5 million miles of black ribbon. Asphalt provides an economical, long-lasting road surface. Asphalt is made up of a binder and an aggregate. The binder is an oil refining byproduct called bituminous. The aggregate is the gravel and sand that is mixed in. An analogy would be chunky peanut butter. The peanut butter would be the binder, and the chunks of peanuts would be the aggregate. While we all know how well peanut butter sticks to the roof of our mouths, it would make a poor road surface. The proper mixture of binder and aggregate is important to the application of asphalt. Temperature is also key. Application temperatures of asphalt should be not less than 250deg and not more than 375deg. The exact temperature is determined by the engineer at the job site. If it's too hot,

An engineer takes a reading of the freshly laid mat of asphalt. Today's temperature is just under 300 degrees, an ideal temperature for compacting. Asphalt is perishable and must be applied and compacted at certain temperatures to provide a good road surface.

carbonized particles will form, and if the temperature is too low it will not compact properly. Most states restrict asphalt paving to days when temperatures are above 40deg Fahrenheit. As we all know, road building and repair are limited to the warmer months. As someone in the Midwest once joked, "We have two seasons, winter and road repair."

After the excavation crews have spent months clearing, cutting, filling, compacting, and grading, it's time for the finished product. The road base must be properly compacted and free of any organic growth. A properly compacted roadbed will be to a depth of over two feet. Compaction prevents the road from sinking into a soft area. Any organic growth left will continue to grow and eventually take the smooth road and make it uneven. The grade and slope must be correct for proper drainage. The problem is laying down an even thickness of asphalt across the entire lane, and doing it consistently and seamlessly across multiple lanes for miles. Specialized machines built exactly for that purpose are simply known as pavers. Their job is to take the hot

Above, this long pile of asphalt is called a windrow. It has been dropped into the path of the paver for pickup. It will soon become a California freeway.

Left, the fresh mat of asphalt, just laid down, is being checked for proper depth by a worker with a ruler. Paving is hot, smelly work. The asphalt is delivered at around 300 degrees. The paver gets very warm from processing the hot asphalt. The sun beats down on the black pavement and warms your feet as you walk. Unfortunately the operator has moved out from under the shade of the umbrella to the right side to carefully steer along the previously laid mat. While not easy work, most paving crew members find this work very rewarding. There is a great deal of teamwork among the paving crew, and there is the satisfaction of taking your kids or grandkids for a ride down a road you paved.

mix asphalt and spread it evenly and consistently across the area to be paved. Uniformity of the aggregate mix, temperature, depth, slope, and grade are all carefully controlled.

A paver is a machine which distributes the hot mix asphalt over the area to be paved. Most pavers are self-propelled by either crawler treads or rubber tires. Less common

Next page, the hopper on this paver is being directly filled by the dump truck. This hopper can hold fourteen tons of asphalt.

The 22in diameter solid rubber front wheels on this Blaw-Knox paver are mounted on an oscillating bogie frame. They provide the steering and support for the hopper.

are the pavers which are towed by other machines. Pavers are rated by the width of pavement they can apply. The paving widths range from a minimum of 4ft to a maximum of 40ft. All pavers are designed to accommodate adjustable paving widths. The most common pavers are adjustable between eight and twelve feet of paving width. The other important specifications of a paver are maximum paving depth and paving speed. Maximum depths of paving range from four inches to twelve inches. Maximum paving speed is slightly over 690ft per minute. In the front of

the paver is the hopper where the hot mix asphalt is dumped. This hopper can hold over fourteen tons of hot mix. At the bottom of the hopper is a conveyor system which feeds two augers at the rear. These augers spread the asphalt across the screed. A screed is the rearmost section of the paver that lays down and irons out the asphalt.

It takes a minimum of three people to run a paver: the operator and two screed men.

Right, this pickup machine is in the process of consuming a windrow and providing the asphalt to the paver's hopper.

Operators of the rollers and the paver discuss the night's paving work about to begin. Operators enjoy working at night. Cool air and the lack of indignant, inconvenienced drivers make for a pleasant working environment.

There is also a crew supporting them by directing trucks and using asphalt rakes. The operator's job is to steer the paver and keep the paving speed constant. While it can pave at a higher rate, the preferred rate is between sixty and eighty feet-per-minute. The job of the screed men is to keep the newly laid mat of asphalt at a constant depth. They stand on the screed, make precise adjustments to the screed, and keep a constant watch on depth. Once the paver converts the truck load of hot mix to a smooth mat of asphalt, a team of rollers will come in to turn it into a road.

The first mechanized pavers were used in the thirties and were very effective for their day. Today's pavers are a godsend to the paving contractor. They are reliable and highly productive. There is nothing that can raise the blood pressure of a contractor more than to have a paver break down with thousands of tons of costly hot mix on the way. Asphalt is a perishable product. It becomes long-lasting only after it has been properly applied and compacted.

The machines, however, are nothing without the men and women of the paving team. Each has a specific job and, when done well, this team of paver crew and roller operators produces a beautiful band of black road. A good crew can lay down 3,000 tons in one shift. That tonnage can increase where the paving season is short and the work days last

The lower area in the rear of the paver is called the screed. It contains the augers that distribute the hot asphalt in an even layer. The men at each end are called screed men. It is their job to make sure the depth is consistent. This screed man is checking depth with a simple tool. Barely visible is the string line that sets the grade along the side of the road.

as long as fourteen hours. Because of the nature of asphalt, the crews don't stop for lunch—they eat on the go. It's also not unusual for the paver to be fueled while running.

I asked one manufacturer about his most unusual paving assignment. He said that paving companies prefer large parking lots; no traffic to contend with, and flat as a pancake. The paving of the NASCAR track in Richmond, Virginia was an unusual assignment. Richmond is a 3/4mi, "D" shaped short track. The front stretch is banked at 8deg, the back stretch 2deg and the corners are banked as high as 16deg. Anyone familiar with racing knows NASCAR stock cars are very tough on tracks. They are very powerful, heavy, and have wide, sticky tires. Turn speeds at Richmond are around 100mph. The challenge at Richmond was to lay a smooth, seamless mat that could withstand the rigors of racing. The paving crews were brought in early to get accustomed to the high banks and to work out any possible problems. One problem was the steep banking. To keep the paver from sliding down the banking, a grader was brought in and, using its blade to steady the paver, both machines drove around the track together. This is yet another example of the teamwork required in the road construction business.

What is Macadam?

The somewhat archaic word "macadam" is often used to describe a smooth roadway of any type. The word macadam comes from the name of Englishman, John McAdam. In 1783, he was appointed to the thankless task of highway commissioner. The word "highway" was a misnomer to describe what was really a series of mud paths. McAdam set out to learn everything he could about roads. Over the years his expertise grew and in 1816 he published *Remarks on the Present System of Road Making*. In his book, he detailed the formula for a durable, low-cost road. His formula was simple: pay strict attention to grading, material selection, and proper drainage. One of his major contributions was the use of a water-bound dust surface. That water-bound surface then progressed to tar-bound, as rubber tires and higher speeds prevailed.

The first macadam road in the United States was built in 1823. It was a ten-mile stretch of road in Maryland between Hagerstown and Boonesboro built by John Davis. Davis's orders to his workers were to use no stone in the roadbed larger than six ounces or two inches in diameter. This first layer was then packed by a six-ton cast iron roller, pulled by a team of horses. McAdam's recommendation was to let the passage of traffic pack the roadbed, but Davis's schedule required a more expedient method. The second layer of stratum was laid in the same fashion as the first, followed by yet a third layer. The finished road was fifteen inches thick in the center and twelve inches thick at the edges. This varied from McAdam's specification, which called for a constant thickness of ten inches.

Two years following the construction in Maryland, the macadam technique was used for a seventy-three-mile stretch of the Cumberland Road. Known for low-cost and durability, the macadam road was the first step in modern American road construction.

Aimed in the direction of its next paving assignment, this Blaw-Knox PF-180H paver waits for an asphalt delivery. The road ahead has been prepared by milling to establish the proper grade and to smooth any irregularities. It has a tack coat of liquid asphalt which aids in adhesion of the finished asphalt mat. The flat black area extending down the road is a reinforcing fabric sometimes called petromat. This mat covers the milled road and covers any cracks, preventing them from migrating up into the new layer of asphalt.

Chapter 8

Rollers & Compactors— Where A Breakdown Is Good

To the casual observer a roller is a roller. They have big steel wheels and probably weigh a lot. They finish asphalt and are simple to operate; just don't drop your watch in front of one. But there's a lot more to rollers than meets the eye. First of all, there are two categories of rollers and compactors: static and vibratory. Also, they come equipped with either steel rollers, tires, or a mix of both. Each is designed for a specific task. Wheeled compactors having a combination of steel drum up front and tires in the rear are used prior to paving for soil compaction. Rollers with two steel rollers and those with all rubber tires are used for the finishing of asphalt. More important, as you will see, is the skill of the operator. As with any piece of construction equipment, they can be high production tools or implements of mass

destruction. A seasoned operator can save the contractor thousands of dollars.

Wheeled compactors are used for the compaction of the dirt that will be the foundation of a road. Wheeled compactors have a pair of rubber tires in the rear and a steel drum vibratory roller in the front. The vibrating roller effectively increases the weight of the machine, thereby accelerating compaction. As an area is filled by the scrapers and leveled by the graders, the compactors come in to compact the soil. The compactors make several passes over the same area to fully compact the soil. The area is watered down to aid in the compaction. Layer after layer of soil is added and compacted to a rate of 95% of its compressibility. This layering and compacting is done to a depth of 2.5ft below grade to provide a solid base for the pavement. Graders work with the compactors, constantly adjusting the grade as the soil is compacted. This provides a smooth surface that won't turn into a series of dips and rises in a few years. Once the road base is compacted and graded, the pavers and finish compactor rollers take over.

This Ingersol-Rand Pro-Pac 115 tips the scales at a little over 25,000lbs. Its vibratory drum can exert an effective rolling/compacting weight of 55,000lbs. The operator has a dial at his finger tips to vary the frequency between 1,000 and 1,890 vibrations per minute (VPM). The VPM is set to match the resonate frequency of the type of soil being compacted.

This rubber-tired compactor is classified as a pneumatic compactor. Its rubber tires work the asphalt into a stable, less permeable surface. It rides on nine high-pressure slick tires.

After a surface of hot mix asphalt (often called a lift or a mat) is laid down by a paver, there are three rollers assigned the task of finishing the job. The first, and probably most important, is the breakdown roller. No, it doesn't breakdown! It breaks down and compacts the asphalt. It is a vibratory type with two steel drums for rolling. Inside each drum is a vibrator mechanism. With the vibrator on, a fifteen-ton roller can have the effective weight of a thirty-three-ton roller. Operator settings control the vibration in both amplitude and frequency. There are several settings for amplitude (the harshness of the vibration) and fre-

This steel wheel roller is the third and final roller/compactor to work this surface. This roller does not have a vibratory system; instead it relies on its weight and smooth rollers to finish this asphalt surface into a beautiful road.

quency (vibrations-per-minute). Asphalt compaction requires high frequency and low amplitude. Riding on one of these compactors is smooth until the operator turns on the vibrator. I was sure my fillings were working their way out of my molars; everything vibrates! The operator must know what he or she is doing, or the newly laid mat can be destroyed. The asphalt needs to be compacted as soon as possible after being laid down by the paver. The temperature of the pavement must be above 250deg, typically between 280 and 300deg.

Above, with its pneumatic rubber tires in the rear, this Bomag BW213D is designed for the compaction of soil only. The rolling width is 82.7in. The operator stops for a short chat with a fellow worker. Notice the sturdy rollover protection for the operator.

Left, not all rollers are big and beefy. This little guy is used for small patching jobs.

This Ingersol-Rand vibratory compactor is called a "breakdown" compactor because it breaks down and compacts the hot asphalt. Large tanks at both ends of this Ingersol-Rand vibratory compactor roller contain water that is sprayed onto the rollers. This keeps the hot asphalt from sticking to them. The operator's seat swivels a full 180 degrees to give the operator the comfort of many seating positions.

The breakdown compactor rolls from the low side of the slope up. The operator must be very careful about turning the vibrator on and off. The roller must be up to speed before the vibrator is turned on, and the vibrator must be turned off prior to stopping. If the vibrator is turned on while the roller is standing still it will hammer itself into two ruts under the rollers. In front of the lead roller, a small wave of asphalt is created. If the roller operator drives too fast for the type material he is rolling, he will drive over this wave and create a speed bump. When rolling a new mat next to one that has been compacted, the operator must be careful to edge his way in. The first pass is called "pinching the joint." This pass will only cover the three or four inches of the new mat. Each successive pass will extend into that mat by only one foot. This careful rolling will insure a seamless joint between mats. The breakdown roller operator must be careful not to roll the new pavement too much or it will start to crack and break up. Once the temperature of the asphalt begins to fall, excessive rolling will damage the new mat. This damage is not something the following rollers can fix; the mat will need to be replaced.

Following the breakdown roller is another type of compactor. This roller is unique in that it has nine pneumatic rubber tires instead of a pair of steel rollers. The tires are set in one row of four in front and one row of five in the back. They are staggered so that from the front, as you look through the gaps of the front tires, you see the rear tires. These tires have no tread and are as smooth as drag slicks. They are ten-ply and carry 110psi of pressure. All the tires must be within 5psi of each other. This roller weighs in at nine tons. Its job is to seal and further compact the asphalt. The asphalt temperature must be above 180deg. The tires are coated with diesel fuel until they get up to temperature. Once the tires get hot, the roller must stay in constant motion over the hot asphalt, or they will cool, and the asphalt will stick to them.

The sun has just set, and the night paving crew is getting ready for a long night's work. This compactor operator is doing a final pre-flight check.

The final member of the team is the finish roller. Its job is to seal the surface. There are no vibrators, just two smooth steel rollers. This roller works from the high side down, the way water would flow off the surface. This roller provides the final step in the road building process. Properly constructed, the new road will last for many years and provide safe transit for all types of vehicle traffic.

The water spray on this roller is broken; as an alternative, a worker is pouring fuel oil onto the roller to keep the asphalt from sticking.

Compactors work in concert with graders on
the final stages of preparing a road foundation
for paving.

Index